Tears of Love
Hope Amidst Infant Loss

I would like to acknowledge the following:

My husband, Captain John Hodges, for his love, support and encouragement.

Joseph Natoli, composer, performer and National/World Accordion Champion who made the song, "Tears of Love", a reality.

Stacey Bigg, for creating the inspiring illustrations.

Abby Porr, choir director at Church of the Resurrection and vocalist for the song, "Tears of Love".

Randy Johnson, for his invaluable publishing advice.

Thank you all so very much,

Kathy Hodges

Dedicated to my grandsons, Marley and Rhodes

Scan the QR code to view the song

Tears of Love
in Sign Language

Our babies are caressed by God's love,
with visions of eternal peace from above.

God comforts us and says, "Keep your faith firm. They pray for your peace also to return."

*Yes, tears keep flowing, coming as they
do, at unexpected moments as we think
of you.*

You could not stay so we could watch you grow,

but you told us you're OK and your love we know.

❦☙♡❦☙

Our candles shimmer on your precious faces.

❦☙♡❦☙

Our hearts still hurt in so many places,
but Christ's great plan for you still shines through.
With tears of love, we have hopes anew.

In loving
memory

In loving
memory

Dear precious ones, though your earthly lives were short,
you still bring hopeful light into our lives.

Come sit with us and hold our hands again.

You touch our hearts and we say Amen!

Our candles shimmer on your precious faces.

Our hearts still hurt in so many places,
but Christ's great plan for you still shines through.
With tears of love, we have hopes anew.

Matthew 5:4
"Blessed are they who mourn,
for they will be comforted."

Psalm 34:19
"The Lord is close to the broken-hearted,
saves those whose spirit is crushed."

Hebrews 11:1
"Faith is the realization of what is hoped for and
evidence of things not seen."

Roman 15:13
"May the God of hope fill you with all joy and peace
in believing, so that you may abound in hope by the
power of the Holy Spirit."

Psalm 62:6
"My soul, be at rest in God alone, from whom comes
my hope."

John 14:27
"Peace I leave with you, my peace I give to you..."

Personal Reflections:

Five Stones Publishing
randy2905@gmail.com

First Edition

ISBN: 978-1-945423-63-5

Names: Hodges, Kathy, author.
Title: Tears of Love / Kathy Hodges.